JourneyThrough®
Romans

50 Devotional Insights by **David Cook**

Discovery House is affiliated
with Our Daily Bread Ministries.

Requests for permission to quote
from this book should be directed to:
Permissions Department
Discovery House
P.O. Box 3566
Grand Rapids, MI 49501
Or contact us by email at
permissionsdept@dhp.org

This Discovery House edition is published with the permission of 10Publishing (UK),
which previously published *Romans: Momentous News* and holds the publishing
licence to the original work. 10Publishing is a division of 10ofthose.com.

Design by Joshua Tan
Typeset by Grace Goh

ISBN 978-1-62707-844-3

Printed in USA
First Printing in 2017

Foreword

Martin Luther believed that the test of maturity of any believer or any church was their understanding of Paul's letter to the Romans.

Over the next fifty days, I pray that you will be impressed afresh with God's perfect plan in bringing us, the unrighteous ones, to God through His Son Jesus Christ, the Righteous One. Romans shows us that there is a world of difference between trying to do what religion requires of us to satisfy God's righteous requirements, and trusting in what God has done to bridge the gulf between Him and us.

The world needs to hear how people can be in the right with God, and we need to see how righteousness is lived out in practice.

I trust that your reading over the next fifty days will start you on an exciting journey of becoming a regular, careful, prayerful reader of God's Word—the Bible.

All Glory to Him,
David Cook

We're glad you've decided to join us on a journey into a deeper relationship with Jesus Christ!

For over sixty years, we have been known for our daily devotional, *Our Daily Bread*. Many readers enjoy the pithy, inspiring, and relevant articles that point them to God and the wisdom and promises of His unchanging Word.

Building on the foundation of *Our Daily Bread*, we have developed this devotional series to help believers spend time with God in His Word, book by book. We trust this daily meditation on God's Word will draw you into a closer relationship with Him through our Lord and Savior, Jesus Christ.

How to use this resource

READ: This book is designed to be read alongside God's Word as you journey with Him. It offers explanatory notes to help you understand the Scriptures in fresh ways.

REFLECT: The questions are designed to help you respond to God and His Word, letting Him change you from the inside out.

RECORD: The space provided allows you to keep a diary of your journey as you record your thoughts and jot down your responses.

An Overview

Paul probably wrote the letter of Romans in about AD 57, towards the end of his third missionary journey (Acts 18:23–19:41), perhaps while he was in Corinth.

This letter has been called the greatest theological document ever written. In it, Paul outlines what Christians believe and explains God's perfect plan in bringing sinners back to Him. It offers Paul's fullest exposition on the all-important issue of righteousness: how a person can be in a right standing with God, and how a person can live a God-honoring righteous life.

The structure of the book reflects this theme:

1:1–17	Introducing the theme of righteousness
1:18–3:20	The natural unrighteousness of humankind
3:21–5:21	How God makes us righteous
6:1–8:39	The key to righteous living
9:1–11:36	God's righteous dealing with Israel
12:1–15:13	Communal righteousness
15:14–16:27	Concluding remarks

Key verses: For I am not ashamed of the gospel, because it is the power of God that brings salvation to everyone who believes: first to the Jew, then to the Gentile. For in the gospel the righteousness of God is revealed—a righteousness that is by faith from first to last, just as it is written: "The righteous will live by faith." —Romans 1:16–17

Read Romans 1:1–7

In these verses, Paul introduces himself, his message, and his readers. The letter begins starkly: "Paul, a servant."

A servant was without rights in the ancient world; a servant's marriage and family were not recognized; a servant's death went uninvestigated. To be a servant was a terrible thing.

However, Paul uses the title as a badge of honor, for he is Jesus Christ's servant. To be the servant of Jesus Christ is a liberating thing.

Note that Paul's description of himself in verses 1 and 5 is a description of how he has been shaped and affirmed by the gospel.

In verses 2 to 4, Paul describes his message. Essentially, the gospel is all about "Jesus Christ our Lord." In verse 3, Paul tells us that Jesus's humanity is real, not imagined. In verse 4, he reminds us that Jesus's deity is confirmed by His bodily resurrection.

In verses 6 to 7, Paul describes his readers according to the gospel's work in them. They are "called" (v. 6); they are "loved by God"; and they are "his holy people" (v. 7).

In verse 7, Paul changes the traditional greeting of "joy and prosperity" to the more gospel-focused "grace and peace." In these introductory verses:

• Paul describes the Scriptures (v. 2), the Spirit (v. 4), and God's people (v. 7) as "holy."

• Here, as in the rest of the New Testament, "holy people"—or "saints" in the other Bible versions—is always used in the plural. The word is derived from the word *holy* and means "set apart, separate."

• Paul forms his self-image and the way he sees others from the gospel. This, according to theologian J. I. Packer in *Knowing God*, is our identity: "I am a child of God. God is my Father; heaven is my home; every day is one day nearer. My Savior is my brother; every Christian is my brother too." It is an identity shaped by the gospel.

How carefully do you
form your self-image
around the gospel's
affirmation of who
you are in Christ?

Are you determined
to see and treat
others as God
sees them? What
difference will
this make to your
relationships?

Read Romans 1:8–17

Paul planted significant churches within the Roman Empire—at Thessalonica, Corinth, and Ephesus—but he did not plant the church at Rome, the center of the Roman Empire.

He had not met the church at Rome. Yet we see his real interest in the progress of its believers. Paul gives thanks for them (v. 8) and prays for them as if they were his responsibility (vv. 9–10). He is a man of generous spirit and is not given to narrow interests. If God is at work, Paul prays for and supports the work. What a model he is in ministry— in contrast to other examples of professional jealousy and territorial insecurity. Paul's attitude provides a necessary corrective.

How often are our sharp criticisms of other ministries simply a thin veneer for envy?

Whether God does His work through Paul or not, Paul rejoices that God's work is being done. He gives thanks and prays in particular that "the way may be opened" (v. 10) so that he could go to them.

Paul wants the work to continue growing, and he wants to impart "some spiritual gift" (v. 11)— probably the gospel—so they will be strengthened.

Paul, however, is not going as a superior. Verse 12 makes it clear that he expects mutual blessing in the visit—note the emphasis on "you and I," "mutually," and "each other's."

There is no aura of detached self-sufficiency about Paul. Some people were alleging that he had not visited the church at Rome because he was not interested in them; he corrects that in verse 13. His desire is for a harvest in Rome among the Gentiles because he is the apostle to the Gentiles (Acts 9:15). It is apparent that besides being a great theologian, Paul was also a passionate missionary and evangelist.

Reflect on Paul's generosity of spirit and his enthusiastic support of gospel work. Are you challenged by his attitude and his activities towards people he had never met?

John Wesley said that parochialism, a narrow-minded view, has always been the enemy of the gospel. In what ways does parochialism creep into your thinking?

Read Romans 1:8–17

Paul concludes the introduction to his letter with three "I am" statements in verses 14, 15, and 16.

First, he says "I am a debtor" (v. 14). He is obligated (literally, indebted) to "Greeks and non-Greeks"—that is, to all cultures—and to "the wise and the foolish"—that is, to all classes within those cultures.

What was the source of this obligation? It came from God's grace to Paul. Once he was the persecutor of the church. Now he is Christ's apostle. Such grace rendered Paul a debtor to all people.

Grace can't be earned. But receiving it so freely puts us under obligation to all. Paul probably felt more at home with people from a similar background to himself, but his sense of obligation is extended to everyone without discrimination.

That is why he says "I am so eager" (v. 15). "Eager" is a rare word in the New Testament. It means, literally, to be single-minded. Such a mind is the essence of maturity. See, for example, Philippians 3:15, where Paul says that those who are mature will express an eagerness of mind in pursuing greater intimacy with Christ and conformity to Christ. Contrast that with the picture of immaturity given in Ephesians 4:14, where immature believers are described as being "tossed back and forth," moving from one novelty to the next. Bible commentator F. F. Bruce says of Paul: "He strikes us as a man possessed of an uncommon strength of will," such is his eagerness to preach the gospel in Rome.

Finally, Paul says, "I am not ashamed" (Romans 1:16). Far from being ashamed of the gospel, Paul is ready to share its message because it is the power of God to bring people to salvation. Its scope is "everyone." It is received by faith; works do not earn it.

Paul longs to go to Emperor Nero's Rome as an ambassador of this gospel. He will not go with a large entourage. He will not go with conventional weaponry. He will go with a message. It is a message about a crucified Jew. In Nero's Rome, this message must have seemed laughable, yet the historian T. R. Glover said that the day would come when men would call their dogs "Nero" and their sons "Paul."

How has your experience of God's grace led you to recognize your obligations?

How does your sense of indebtedness show itself in your giving, your praying, and your activities? Does being unashamed of the gospel lead you to share it with others?

Day 4

Read Romans 1:8–17

Most commentators agree that verses 16 and 17 constitute the theme of the letter.

Verse 17 tells us that the gospel reveals "the righteousness of God." Righteousness is normally used to speak of a relationship that is right. However, Paul may also be speaking here of the righteous character of God—that God is just. When the gospel is preached, it reveals God's justice and yet, at the same time, it also reveals God's mercy. It shows how sinful humans can have a right relationship with Him.

Paul makes it clear that this relationship is by faith, not earned. He quotes Habakkuk 2:4, that those who are righteous live simply by their faithfulness—by trusting God.

Martin Luther, the sixteenth-century Augustinian monk, was haunted by God's righteousness and by his own sin. He tried every means the church offered in his quest for peace with God. "I greatly longed to understand Romans and nothing stood in the way but that one expression, 'the justice of God,' because I took it to mean that justice whereby God is just and deals justly in punishing the unjust. My situation was that, although an impeccable monk, I stood before God as a sinner troubled in conscience . . . Then I grasped that the justice of God is that righteousness by which, through grace and sheer mercy, God justifies us through faith. Then I felt myself to be reborn and to have gone through open doors into paradise."

Luther went on to lecture on Romans and to write a commentary on it. It was on hearing a public reading of the introduction to Luther's commentary that John Wesley, founder of the Methodist movement, felt his heart "strangely warmed" and was converted. Here is a truth that has changed the course of history, a righteousness coming to us by grace, through faith, based on the finished work of Jesus Christ. This is what the gospel and "the righteousness of God" is all about.

What does it mean in your life each day to enjoy a right relationship with God—not because it has been earned or through merit, or even because of faith, but all because of Jesus?

Why do you think seeking to win God's favor by religious activity is both impossible and unnecessary?

Day 5

Read Romans 1:18–32

Good news, bad news! Paul gives us the bad news first. (In fact, the bad news doesn't conclude until 3:21.)

God's wrath is the bad news. The reason for His wrath is people's godlessness and wickedness, as seen in their suppression of the truth (v. 18). The truth is suppressed because of a determined, rebellious will. Verses 19 to 20 tell us that people know about God's power and deity by observation of the created order. However, they deliberately suppress the truth about God by exchanging the truth and glory of God for the lie of idolatry (vv. 23, 25).

The proper response to God is to glorify Him and to give Him thanks. Instead, people worship and serve created things rather than the Creator (vv. 23, 25).

What is the nature of God's wrath? Verses 24, 26, and 28 say that God "gave them over." God leaves humanity to live with the fruit of its choice. This fruit comprises general uncleanness (v. 24), shameful lusts and perverse sexual activity (vv. 26–27), and living contrary to God's standard (vv. 28–32). Such a lifestyle becomes, therefore, the judgment of God. It is ironic that our society describes as "gay" a lifestyle characterized by a desperate search for the fulfillment of lusts, which ought never—and will never—be satisfied.

God "gave them over." How different to His judgment on Ananias and Sapphira (Acts 5), which was swift and obvious, removing their hypocrisy from the church. This "giving over" is a less obvious and more passive form of wrath. It allows sin to meander on through the life of the church, and it makes life hard for God's people.

Yet, mercifully, an opportunity for repentance and salvation is provided.

How often do we get sidetracked by the symptoms and not look for the root cause as to why the world is the way it is?

People act the way they do (vv. 24–32) because of a theological infection: they suppress the truth of God in favor of idols (vv. 18, 23, 25). The appropriate antibiotic for such an infection is theological: only the gospel provides the cure. What are the implications of this truth?

Read Romans 2:1–16

n these verses, Paul shifts attention from the pagan idolater to the self-righteous moralist. He shows that passing judgment on others does not exempt a person from God's wrath (vv. 1–3). Passing judgment is mentioned five times.

God is kind, tolerant, and patient. Yet, if the moralist interprets this as approval of his or her lifestyle, that attitude builds up cardiac sclerosis—a hardening of the heart (v. 5). God's kindness and patience are designed to lead the unrepentant to repentance (v. 4). Peter echoes this thought in 2 Peter 3:9.

Additionally, the Lord makes it clear that calamities remind us that we are living in rebellion against God in a post-garden of Eden environment (Luke 13:1–5). Calamities are meant to lead us to repentance.

Thus God speaks one message to the world: When things are good, repent; when things are disastrously bad, repent.

Repentance involves a complete change of attitude and action. It means turning away from rebelling against or ignoring God's claim upon us, and recognizing that claim and serving Him in reverence.

This is precisely what the self-righteous moralist does not do. He or she has nothing to repent about; he or she is storing up God's wrath for the day it will be revealed (v. 5). We are lost because God's justice dispenses punishment on the basis of our sinful acts.

Verses 7 to 11 are the most difficult verses of the letter. This is because they appear to contradict its central message—that we are justified not by works but through faith. But Paul does not contradict himself. Neither does he speak hypothetically.

Paul is clear that God does not have one standard for the Jew and a different one for the Gentile—God does not play favorites (v. 11). Paul gives the following affirmation: Judgment is based on works; it is universal; and it is individual. There is one standard and only one. God will not be fooled by the hypocritical judgments made by self-righteous people on others. He will not be swayed by our moralizing or by our condemnation of others. God is interested in what we do (v. 6), for it reveals who we are.

Where do you stand in the light of God's judgment?

In what ways might you have thought too highly of yourself? What are the things listed at the end of Romans 1 that you think you would never do?

Day 7

Read Romans 2:1–16

Although Paul doesn't mention the legalistic Jew specifically until Romans 2:17, he probably has such a person in mind as he addresses the hypocritical, self-righteous attitude of the moralist in 2:1.

"God does not show favoritism" (v. 11). When judgment comes, it will be impartial (v. 6). In these verses, Paul echoes Peter's conviction about God's impartiality at the time of Cornelius's conversion (Acts 10:34–35). Paul stresses God's impartiality in Romans 2:9–10 with his repetition of the phrase, "first for the Jew, then for the Gentile."

So those whose hearts are set for glory, honor, and immortality (v. 7) will be given eternal life, whether they are Jew or non-Jew. Similarly, those who live for self, reject truth, and follow evil will know wrath, trouble, and distress (v. 9).

In verses 12 to 16, Paul shows that God will judge people by their actions. They will also be held accountable for the truth they possessed. All people (Jew or non-Jew) know something of God (1:19–20), and therefore all people have a sense of right and wrong. Such truth as people possess will provide their definition of sin. People will be judged for sin, either sin as defined by Moses's law, or sin as defined by conscience. Paul shows that an inner morality is evident in the Gentiles who, without having Moses's law, often naturally do the things required by that law (vv. 14–15). On judgment day (as Paul indicated in verse 16), their thoughts will accuse and excuse them when they realize it was God's law they were disobeying and obeying.

Remember, Paul is showing here how people are lost, not how they are saved. We will be judged by what we do in the light of what we know, whether it is the law of Moses (as in the case of the Jew) or the law of conscience (as in the case of the Gentile). Universally, we will be found to be sinners who have acted contrary to the standard we possess.

Only the gospel, which Paul comes to in 3:21, will be able to give relief to all of us who are under the threat of God's wrath because of our sin.

There are those who say that a pagan is better off without the gospel. Let the pagan stand before God to be judged in the light of what he or she knew, for if the pagan hears and rejects the gospel, he or she will be condemned for that. Do you agree?

What part are you playing in seeing the gospel taken to the world? How does it affect the way you give, pray, and live?

Read Romans 2:17–28

While Paul has the Jews in view as he pens Romans 1–2:16, he now has the Jews specifically in mind.

God entrusted the Jews with the law. However, Paul makes it clear that mere possession of the law does not qualify one to be a guide, a light, an instructor, or a teacher (vv. 19–20). If the law is not lived, God is dishonored (vv. 21–23). Verse 24 is heavy in its condemnation that "God's name is blasphemed among the Gentiles" because of the lawless lives led by the Jews, God's people.

Paul then turns from the law to the issue of circumcision and its inner, spiritual meaning. He argues that just as mere possession of the law is no protection against God's condemnation, circumcision is of value only if it indicates a circumcised heart. A noncircumcised Gentile who keeps the law and lives as though he were circumcised, will condemn the disobedient, circumcised Jew (v. 27). Jewishness is not outward and physical; it is inward and spiritual. It is a circumcision of the heart (see Deuteronomy 10:16; Jeremiah 9:26; and John 8:39–45).

Thus the Jew who depends on the superiority of having God's law and the mark of the covenant in his flesh is in for a big surprise. Unless these outward signs are matched by inward experience and integrity, they are empty. (Paul illustrates this truth later in the case of Abraham, 4:11.)

The application to the issue of sacraments is obvious. Sacraments are empty signs if they are not matched by the inner reality they symbolize. Baptism, the initiating rite, is a symbol of our new birth, our death with Christ, and our resurrection to new life. The Lord's Supper is a reminder of the foundation of our right relationship with God through the work of His Son on the cross. Unless these truths are real in our experience, participation in the sacraments is of no use.

Paul's concern is to show how Jews are lost. Jews are lost because of their disregard for God's lordship in their lives. No amount of religious activity can compensate for that before God.

What about your heart? Is it right with God? This is an important question to answer today!

Think about how you may be tempted to put your faith in doing good things, even things like this Bible-reading time, rather than in Christ for a relationship with God.

Day 9

Read Romans 3:1–8

I, as far as God is concerned, Jews are no better off than anyone else, what advantage is there in being a Jew, one of God's people?

Paul says the advantages are many, although he lists only one (v. 2). "Jews have been entrusted with the very words of God," the Old Testament Scriptures. Israel's supreme privilege is that she was the first to know the mind of God.

Paul anticipates two other questions. The first is in verses 3 to 4. Does Jewish unfaithfulness release God from His obligation to be faithful? "No way!" says Paul. "God always remains faithful." John Calvin, the sixteenth-century theologian, said that this is "the primary axiom of all Christian philosophy." God is faithfully committed to His Word.

King David acknowledged that God was just to punish him for his sin (v. 4, see Psalm 51:4). God is therefore faithful. He stands by His covenant promises and His covenant threats. His faithfulness is seen in His punishment of David and in His punishment of Jewish faithlessness.

The second question comes in verses 5 to 8. If God's faithfulness is shown when He punishes our sin, then why not continue sinning? Isn't God unjust to punish us when our sin highlights His faithfulness? "Certainly not!" Paul responds strongly (v. 6). If that were the case, God could never judge us. Notice here how Paul accepts God's judgment as a fact. It is immovable. Your thinking is wrong if it rules out God's judgment.

Paul says that those who justify sinning because it enhances God's character are justly condemned (v. 8). Paul had been slandered; it was claimed he encouraged sin, no doubt because of his emphasis on faith, not works. Others were not slandered like this, no doubt because their version of the gospel had an element of human contribution to it.

In the endeavor to justify ourselves and condemn God, we see the depth of sin in the human heart.

If a doctrine causes us to have a slack attitude towards sin and to live below God's moral standard, then it is not the truth. It is not of God.

The condemnation of the Jew is a reminder to us that one can be zealous, knowledgeable, and religious, and yet not know God. Do you know God or merely know about God?

Day 10

Read Romans 3:9–20

Following the rabbis' pattern of substantiating their case by a list of Old Testament Scriptures, Paul quotes from Psalms, Ecclesiastes, and Isaiah to summarize his argument about the state of humanity.

The repetition of "no one," "not even one," "no one," "no one," "not even one," stands out in verses 10 to 12. There are no exceptions; we are all worthless. The word used is of "milk gone bad." Having been created for a relationship with God, none of us has this relationship with Him or displays any sign of seeking it.

This lack of relationship with God, or righteousness, is evident in our conduct. What stands out in verses 13 to 17 is the prominence of the throat, tongue, lips, and mouth.

The mouth is the accurate indicator of the state of the heart (Matthew 12:34). The tongue is shown to be full of cursing, uncleanness, destruction, and deceit, and our activities parallel our words (Romans 3:15–17). To explain the reason for this, Paul quotes from Psalm 36:1, "There is no fear of God before their eyes" (v. 18). And the eyes are the windows to the soul. The concluding summary of 1:18–3:20 is stated in verses 19 to 20. The law, God's unchangeable standard, silences all excuses. Bible commentator J. B. Phillips renders these verses as, "It is the straight edge of the Law that shows us how crooked we are." The law makes us conscious of our sin. What the law will not do is provide a right standing with God through observance of its requirements.

God, therefore, justly condemns humanity, and there is no way out. We cannot work our way into heaven; any solution must come from God's side. We do not like to face the reality of ourselves. It is like looking at an unflattering photo—we protest about the bad focus. But here is God's perfectly focused photograph of ourselves.

It is important for us to be convicted about our hopeless state if we are to appreciate fully the wonder of the good news of salvation.

Think about
your growth in
knowledge. How
well do you know
yourself?

What did Jesus
know that kept Him
from trusting people
(John 2:24–25)?
Reflect on
Jeremiah 17:9.

Day 11

Read Romans 3:21–26

According to Bible scholar Leon Morris, this is perhaps the most significant paragraph ever written.

After the bleak but realistic news of 1:18–3:20, we come to the momentously good news: That a right standing with God, apart from human performance, has been revealed. It comes to all who believe in the faithful work of Jesus Christ (vv. 21–22).

The need for such a relationship is universal (v. 23). In explaining this, Paul employs three words in common use in his time.

"Justified" (v. 24): This is a legal word whereby God, the judge, declares the guilty sinner to be in the right with Him. How can God do this and remain just? He does it on the basis of Jesus's death, which has fully paid our penalty and acquitted us.

"Redemption" (v. 24): This is a word from commerce. It is what Jesus's death means to us—He buys us back for God, paying the ransom price of His own perfect life.

"Sacrifice of atonement" (v. 25), or "propitiation": This is a religious word which explains what Jesus's death means to God. Through His death, Jesus absorbs the wrath of God due to our sin so that we don't have to take the punishment we deserve.

Thus God the Father, in the death of the Son, makes His attitude to sin patently clear (v. 25). God also demonstrates His justice (v. 26). His perfect Son gives His life to set us free, in that He absorbs God's just wrath against human sin. God in His love satisfies His own justice, the penalty of sin is paid, and the law is upheld. God is just and is able to be the justifier by declaring us to be in the right because of the work of Jesus.

We are set right not because of our faith; we are set right through faith (v. 22) and by faith (v. 28). Faith links us to the work of Christ, which is the foundation of a right relationship with God.

The foundation of this relationship is the unchanging work of Christ. God is always satisfied with the work of His Son. Hence, our relationship with God is unchanging and stable because it is based on what Jesus has done.

ThinkThrough

In the light of the
truths revealed
in this Scripture
passage, why is
the practice of
religious rituals to
earn God's favor
both impossible and
unnecessary?

Why are these truths
so liberating?

Read Romans 3:27–31

f faith is my response to what God has done, where does faith come from? If it comes from within, if it is my own contribution, then it could become a ground for my boasting.

Paul makes three points regarding justification:

1. Verses 27 to 28: Justification is not earned. It is not based on keeping the law. Justification is through faith, and faith is God's gift. Otherwise justification would be a work. If it was a work, it would provide grounds for boasting. So boasting is excluded.

2. Verses 29 to 30: Justification means that God is not some localized deity having oversight and interest in the Jews alone. Justification is by faith. It is not by keeping the law or circumcision. Faith can be found in either the circumcised Jew or the uncircumcised Gentile.

3. Verse 31: In justification, God does not set aside His own justice. He does not turn a blind eye to our sin and disobedience. He does not nullify the law. Rather, our faith is directed to the work of the One who fulfilled the law's demands. The law is upheld by the provision of a perfect life offered (redemption) and God's just wrath absorbed (propitiation).

Thus, in justification, God is seen to be central. He is the source of faith that we need to link us to the work of Christ. He is the expansive God with no limited national interest. He is totally just and yet, as justifier, He is wonderfully merciful.

The early theologian Saint Augustine prayed, "O God, demand what You will, but supply what You demand!" God demands perfection, and He meets that demand in the provision of His Son.

Do you give God the honor due Him for the fact that you are a believer? See where faith comes from in Hebrews 12:2 and Ephesians 2:8–9. See how a person's conversion is described in John 1:12–13 and Acts 11:18, 13:48, and 16:14. How does this differ from the way we describe the process of a person's conversion?

A former Archbishop of Canterbury, William Temple, said, "All I have to contribute to my own salvation is the sin from which I need to be saved." What does this mean to you?

Day 13

Read Romans 4:1–15

Paul anticipates objections to what he's said about justification through faith. It is so revolutionary that people will think he simply thought it up. Objectors to the gospel today often reject it on the basis that it is just Paul's gospel.

To prove that what he is saying is not innovative, Paul gives two illustrations.

First, he takes us back to the experience of Abraham. He shows that Abraham was not justified by works, or he would have had something to boast about (v. 2). Rather, he quotes Genesis 15:6. Abraham knew the blessing of credited righteousness by faith. This righteousness was unearned. It came as a gift to him through faith (vv. 4–5).

Second, Paul quotes Psalm 32:1–2 to show that even the great King David anticipated the blessing of a covering for sin and that God would not count sins against those who have faith.

Abraham has a credited righteousness, while David's sins are not imputed to David himself. So justification is not new; the experiences of Abraham and David confirm it.

Is this justification for Jews only? This is Paul's next question. His response is "No," because when Abraham received the blessing (Genesis 15), he was uncircumcised. It was not until fourteen years later that his circumcision took place (Genesis 17). Circumcision did not confer the blessing on Abraham; it was the sign and seal (Romans 4:11) of the blessing of credited righteousness. So circumcision does not establish our lineage to Abraham. Ours is a spiritual lineage, faith being the common link. Abraham is the father of those who believe God and so "follow in the footsteps of the faith that our father Abraham had" (v. 12).

The law did not confer the blessing on Abraham either (vv. 13–15). Righteousness was credited to him well before the law was given. The law brings only wrath because it accuses us, and we cannot keep it. Abraham's righteousness was by grace through faith, not by circumcision nor by law-keeping. Consequently, he is the father of all believers in God's promise, the gospel.

As we shall see in verses 16 to 25, **God's method of salvation has never changed. Faith focused on God's gospel is always to be the controlling factor of our lives.** Abraham is our father in this, because for him, as for us, God spoke and man believed. Here is God and man in a right relationship.

The Jews believed that having the law and being circumcised were safe shelters against God's displeasure. In what ways do we substitute other things for the only safe shelter we have for salvation, namely, Jesus?

Day 14

Read Romans 4:16–25

Abraham is the father of all those who have faith. The name "Abraham" means "father of many nations," and that is what he is. Since Abraham is our father, he is our model or pattern. Paul says that the way God relates to Abraham is the way God relates to us.

Paul repeats that Abraham's justification was not earned but was by faith (vv. 16–17). His faith is a model for ours. Its object was the promise of God (v. 18). Faith has no inherent value apart from its object. Bible teacher Paul E. Little said, "A strong faith in a weak bridge will not bridge the gulf, but a weak faith in a strong bridge will get you to the other side."

The strength of faith (vv. 19–20) is seen in how Abraham believed in spite of the seeming impossibility of the promise that the aged Sarah would bear the aged Abraham a son. The focus of his faith was God's ability to do what He said (v. 21). Abraham was not put off, because he was convinced of God's power.

The blessing that flowed was righteousness, credited to him graciously through faith (v. 22). The reason this incident was recorded was not for his sake, but for ours (vv. 23–25)—that just as Abraham believed in the promise of God, so we are to believe in the work of Christ as the basis for our justification.

> Just as Abraham believed God could bring an heir from one as good as dead, so we trust in the God who brought His own Son from death to life.

Verse 25 reminds us that Jesus died because of our sin. His resurrection was like God's confirmation that Jesus's work on the cross had been accepted. Therefore our justification is sure.

Abraham believed the promise of redemption (v. 17), and so do we (v. 24). Abraham looked forward to the blessing that would come to his life (Genesis 12:3); we look back to the Redeemer who came and through whom we are blessed, as was Abraham. Abraham's life was one of great blessing. He had known persecution and harassment, yet God blessed him, and today there are approximately 1.4 billion living sons and daughters of Abraham.

He is indeed our father, our model, and our pattern.

In what way does
Abraham's faith
in God challenge
our own?

Which of God's
promises do you
find hardest to trust
today? Why? How
does Abraham's
example help you?

Day 15

Read Romans 5:1–11

Justification is such a treasure that Paul now outlines the three blessings that flow from it.

First, God is at peace with us because His justice has been satisfied (v. 1). He holds nothing against us.

Second, not only do we have a relationship with God that is absent of anger, but we also have access to a gracious relationship— an unconditional, undeserved relationship with God (v. 1).

Third, we have the certain expectation that, in the future, we will share in the glory of God (v. 2; 8:18). But we not only rejoice in hope, we also rejoice in suffering. Why? Because suffering leads to perseverance, which leads to character. Perseverance in the face of opposition shows the authenticity of our commitment. Such an experience leads to a fresh or new yearning for the fulfillment of our hope (v. 4).

How can we be sure our hope will be fulfilled? Paul gives us three reasons:

- Verse 5: God has given us the Holy Spirit who reminds us of God's love. God's love will not allow the hopes of His children to be disappointed.

- Verses 6 to 8: The objective ground, or proof, of God's love is the cross where Jesus died for our sin (vv. 6, 8). Jesus's death is gracious because those for whom He died are described as sinners, helpless, and enemies. This demonstration of God's love lies at the very core of Christianity, which is about the death of the innocent Son for His undeserving people.

- Verses 9 to 11: Finally, Paul argues that our hope will not be dashed because God reconciled us when we were His enemies. Now that we are His friends, He will surely save us. Having done the greater thing, He will do the comparatively lesser thing—the fulfillment of our hope.

We can be confident that our hope of glorification will not be dashed.

ThinkThrough

God says having two
witnesses in a case
is important (see
Deuteronomy 19:15).
Who are the two
witnesses to God's
love mentioned
here? How are they
different?

What should
the blessings of
justification cause
you to do?

Read Romans 5:12–21

Preacher Martyn Lloyd-Jones calls this section the core of the letter. Here, Paul sums up all that he has said about how God has released us from the penalty for sin. He shows that there were only ever two "camps" with two representatives—Adam (v. 14) and his counterpart Jesus Christ (v. 15). We are represented either by the first Adam or the second Adam.

The first Adam, by an act of disobedience, brought condemnation and death to us all (vv. 16–17). The second Adam, however, brings grace and the gift of righteousness to His people (v. 17).

Paul also shows that the way we are justified parallels the way we were condemned (vv. 18–19). Adam trespassed and we were all condemned (v. 18). Christ obeyed and we were all justified (v. 18). The act of the one renders the many either condemned or justified.

How were we condemned? God imputed to us the disobedience of our representative head, Adam. Before we had actually sinned, Adam's sin was debited to our account. That is why people were condemned before sin was defined by Moses and the law (vv. 12–14). They were condemned because Adam's sin was imputed or attributed to them.

The way we are condemned is, in the case of Christ and the believer, a pattern for our justification. All the righteousness and obedience of Christ was imputed to us. It was credited to our account and we were declared righteous (v. 19).

What then happened to all our debits—Adam's trespass and our personal sin? It was reckoned to Christ's account. He did not become actually sinful any more than we became actually perfect, but, as with a bookkeeping entry, our sin was debited to Him. He died to pay its penalty, and now His righteousness is credited to us (see 2 Corinthians 5:21).

When God looks at our account now, He sees only the accounted perfection of Jesus. Law defined sin and made it obvious, but God's grace in the work of Christ is always sufficient to cover human sin and bring us, through credited righteousness, to eternal life (vv. 20–21).

It is through faith that we transfer from the camp of Adam (the camp of our birth) to the camp of Christ (the camp, according to John, of the children of God). The first camp is by birth, and the second by rebirth (John 1:12–13).

We are reminded in Romans 4:3 and 5:15 that God acts consistently in the Old and New Testaments. The Bible is thus one book of the one God. How does this affect your view of yourself as a believer, and of the Bible as God's Word?

Day 17

Read Romans 6:1–14

Paul anticipates the big question: Since grace increases to cover sin (5:20), why not sin more so that God's grace increases even more? If God sees us perfect because of the work of Jesus, why worry about sin?

Paul responds to any thinking that encourages a slack attitude to sin with "By no means!" (6:2). He goes on to tell us why we are to be holy.

We are to be holy because we died with Christ. His death was a proxy death for us. We were with Him on the cross, with Him in the tomb, and with Him in His resurrection (vv. 3–4). When Christ died for sin, we died to sin. Baptism, Paul says, is a constant reminder of our participation in Christ's death and resurrection. Union with Jesus is the key to our justification and holiness.

When we died with Christ, we died to sin. Sin did not die; rather, our physical body, which sin used as its instrument, was taken out of gear (v. 6). Meanwhile, we have been raised with Christ to a new life (vv. 4, 5, 8). This new life is never-ending (v. 9). Qualitatively, it is a life lived in knowledge of God and in reverence for Him (v. 10).

Significantly, up to this point in the letter, Paul has not given one command. When it comes to justification, we have no contribution to make, so nothing can be commanded of us. But in verses 11 to 14, he gives a number of orders.

The first is attitudinal. We are to make the same calculation about ourselves as God has made about us; that is, we are "dead to sin and alive to God" (v. 11). As God sees us, so we are to see ourselves. Then we do not let sin reign over us (v. 12).

Next, we do not keep going to sin's temple to make offerings there. Rather, we commit ourselves once and for all to God's lordship (v. 13) The reason for this is that we live in a relationship not ruled by observing law or by earning merit. We live in an unconditional, undeserved relationship of grace.

The key to holiness is to recognize our solidarity with Christ and to stop sinning. As we resist temptation, God will help us to resist it (see Philippians 2:12–13).

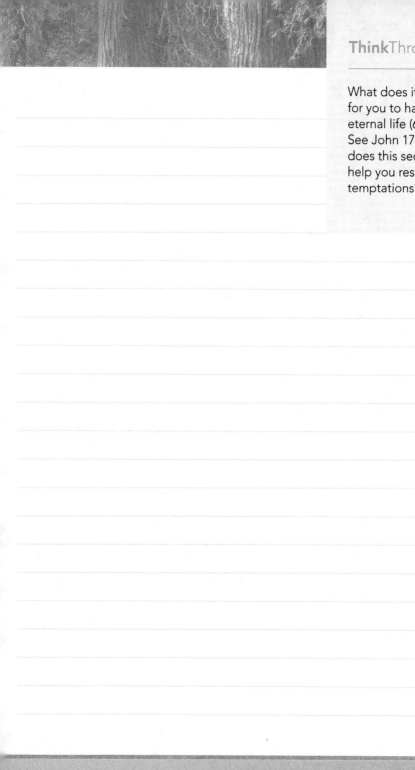

What does it mean for you to have eternal life (6:10)? See John 17:3. How does this section help you resist temptations?

Day 18

Read Romans 6:15–23

Paul is still talking about holiness. Today, he takes us to the slave market. A person can claim to be anyone's slave, but the reality is that the master he obeys enslaves him.

Paul pursues the question of those who are justified and their attitude to sin. There are only two possible masters (v. 16)—sin ("Master Sin") or obedience and righteousness ("Master Righteousness"). The essence of sin, therefore, is disobedience.

Paul further identifies and describes these two masters in verse 19. "Master Sin" pays a wage: it is earned; it is deserved; it is death (vv. 21, 23). Death is separation from God. However, slavery to obedience ("Master Righteousness") brings about a benefit or gift. That benefit is eternal life—life in relationship with God.

Since we were born into slavery to "Master Sin," how did we come to obedience? The answer comes in verse 17. Paul gives thanks to God that "[we] have come to obey from [our] heart the pattern of teaching that has now claimed [our] allegiance."

In other words, this happens when we place our confidence in the gospel. Notice that the gospel was not entrusted to us; we were entrusted to it.

Through the obedience of the gospel that comes from faith (1:5), we come under the shelter and security of the gospel, which now keeps us safe. So why go back to the former master, sin? We owe him nothing. He pays us death, and we are ashamed of what we did when we served him (v. 21).

This is the second image regarding holiness: first, union with Christ in death and resurrection; second, being set free from "Master Sin" and being enslaved to "Master Righteousness" (v. 18).

Verse 23 provides the summary: Sin pays a wage (death); God gives a gift (eternal life). The gift comes to us because of the work of Christ Jesus our Lord. We cannot have life apart from Him.

Sinless perfection is not a reality for life on earth (see 1 John 1:5–10). But do you take your responsibility to resist temptation seriously enough?

Day 19

Read Romans 7:1–13

Paul has used the image of our solidarity with Jesus—we died, we were buried, and we were raised with Him (6:1–14). He has used the image of the master and slave relationship (6:15–23). Now, he uses the image of death (7:1–6).

The point Paul makes is that death frees a person from the binding of the law (v. 3). If a woman's husband dies, she is free to remarry. But if she marries while her husband is still alive, she becomes an adulteress. The difference is that death legitimately terminates marriage.

By dying to the law, the believer is legitimately free to "marry" (that is, to be united with) Christ and thus to serve in the new way of the Spirit (vv. 4–6).

What, then, is our relationship to the law? Do we fear it like the legalist does? Do we hate it like the person who sees the law as the source of his problems? No, we love the law. We do so because it represents the will of God and because Christ kept it. The law is holy and good (v. 13), though it cannot save us. The problem is not the law but our sin (vv. 8–9, 11). The law's role is to identify sin (vv. 7–8) and to show us our condemnation as sinners (vv. 9–11).

When was Paul "alive apart from the law" (v. 9)? It was probably when he believed he had lived consistently with the law (see Philippians 3:6). But when he realized the true jurisdiction of the law, not only over outward actions but also over inner attitudes, he realized how lost he was.

So Paul summarizes: The good law identified sin and condemned him as a sinner (v. 13). In that way, it prepared him for the Savior to come (7:24–25).

The law gets us ready for the coming of Christ by bringing conviction of sin (see Galatians 3:24–25). As law-abiding believers, we love the law yet we recognize its limitation. It cannot save or sanctify us. The problem lies with us. To blame the law, according to Bible commentator F. F. Bruce, is like a prisoner in jail blaming the law which put him there as though it were the law's fault and not his own.

Do you seek to
honor the law as
did our Lord Jesus
Christ?

It is only in the light
of conviction of our
sinfulness that we
realize the greatness
of the rescue we
have in Jesus. How
often do you search
your life in the light
of the law, so as to
realize the extent of
your sinfulness?

Day 20

Read Romans 7:14–25

There are three options for understanding who is described as the "I" in these verses, and of the state he is in.

Option 1: Is Paul speaking of himself as a believer? If so, he is describing normal Christian experience.

Option 2: Is Paul speaking of himself as an "unspiritual" believer? If so, it would introduce an unbiblical third category of person. In addition to the non-Christian and the Christian, there would now be the "semi-Christian."

Option 3: Is Paul describing his experience with the law as a God-fearing Israelite? In this case, the experience he describes—best summarized in verse 19 as "I do not do the good I want to do, but the evil I do not want to do—this I keep on doing"—is the typical experience of every Israelite who seeks to keep God's law as the way to righteousness.

As to these options, look at Romans 9:30–33 and 10:3 to see that the Israelites sought to establish their own righteousness through law-keeping. Paul explains in today's verses and elsewhere that this is an impossible quest. "What a wretched man I am! Who will rescue me from this body that is subject to death?" (v. 24) is the typical cry of the one under law who cannot keep it. Paul sees himself bound to his body of death, a reference to the King Mezentius of Roman mythology who tied living criminals to the decomposing corpses of their victims. The law is good (7:12), but it is powerless to change us or enable us to keep it.

The cry of triumph in verse 25 follows closely on the cry of anguish in verse 24. Chapter 8 fully describes the deliverance we have in Christ, climaxing with our glorification (8:18).

According to the first option, verse 19 is an accurate description of the believer's experience with good and evil. But if this is typical of us, how can the exhortation of 6:19—not to offer our bodies in slavery to wickedness but rather to righteousness—be meaningful, since the normal experience is one of frequent defeat? Also, how can 7:19 and 8:9–11 both be accurate pictures of the believer when they seem to say contrary things? Surely they cannot both be an accurate description of a Christian. The first option does not seem to fit the context of Paul's argument as well as the third one does.

Our performance will not be perfect this side of glory, but the desperate defeat and wretchedness described in these verses is evidence of the law's impotence to save and of the great need of unsaved Israel to come to Christ where there is no condemnation (8:1).

Think about the dilemma of the God-fearer who has God's law and who desires to be obedient, and yet does not know Christ. Thank God for the deliverance we have through Christ from the condemnation we deserve.

Day 21

Read Romans 8:1–17

We come to an especially majestic section of the letter. In it, Paul shows us two things.

First, we are delivered from the just condemnation of the law. The law could not justify us because we could not keep it (v. 3), so God provided His Son who perfectly met the requirements of the law and then took our place as the perfect offering for sin (vv. 3–4).

Second, while the sinful nature of the "old man" remains a powerful force within the believer, God has given the believer a powerful gift—the indwelling Spirit who enables us to do God's will. (There are more references to the Spirit in chapter 8 than in all the other chapters of the letter.)

In verses 5 to 8, Paul contrasts life in the Spirit with life in the flesh.

Being children of God means that we have the Holy Spirit (v. 9). (See Acts 2:38 for the great blessings of the new covenant.)

The Spirit revitalizes our aging, dying bodies (vv. 10–11).

The Spirit leads us to put to death the misdeeds of the body (vv. 14–15). He empowers us for godly living.

The Spirit gives us deep assurance that we are God's children (vv. 15–16).

We can relate to God on the most intimate basis and call Him "Abba Father" (v. 15).

The very essence of being a child is that we have a parent. Since we have a parent, we are heirs and we have an inheritance (v. 17). Here, we are reminded that we are heirs of God our Father and we will share the inheritance with God the Son, our elder brother (v. 29b). However, this inheritance will not be split 50-50. Being a "co-heir" means that everything that is Christ's is ours, so it is 100-100. Our entry to our inheritance is like His. For Him, the inheritance was the crown via the cross; for us, it will be glory via present suffering (v. 17).

Here, Paul answers two questions: Am I condemned by my past life? Does God leave me without resources in the battle with the flesh? The answer to both questions is "No." Because of what Jesus has done, we are not condemned. And because God has given us His Holy Spirit, we are not without resources.

Knowing that we are co-heirs with Christ and thus possess the hope of inheritance, how can you encourage this hope to be more dominant in your thinking?

The Puritans thought about heaven on a daily basis. Why? (See 1 Thessalonians 1:3.) Do you?

Day 22

Read Romans 8:18–27

As children of God, we are waiting for our promised inheritance (v. 17). What is our present experience as we wait?

First, Paul says it is one of suffering (v. 18). In verse 35, he outlines what he has in mind. He tells us that not only do we groan under the weight of present suffering (v. 23), but the whole of creation also groans under the frustration of its generation-growth-decay cycle. Creation is waiting for its liberation from the bondage of this cycle, and that will happen when the sons of God are revealed, that is, when Christ returns (v. 19).

We have received the downpayment of our salvation in the person of the Holy Spirit (v. 23). We groan as we wait for the rest of the payment, when our bodies will be transformed (1 Corinthians 15:35).

Our present experience is one of suffering and groaning. Paul says there should be none of the unreal positivism that dominates some churches which claim the experience of life is one triumph after another. Note also that there is none of the constant gloom that may suit some personalities, for we are not as we were before we were believers.

We have received the Holy Spirit, the downpayment, the firstfruits that guarantee our "adoption to sonship," and "the redemption of our bodies" (v. 23).

Secondly, Paul says our experience involves weakness (v. 26). This is not a moral weakness, but the weakness of ignorance. Sometimes life is so complex that we simply do not know the appropriate things to pray for. However, the downpayment, the Spirit, does know. He intercedes effectively for us in a way that is consistent with God's will when we may not know what God's will is in a situation (v. 27).

So here is our present experience—realistic yet not one of unrelieved gloom, for through the work of Jesus, God has given us His Holy Spirit. The Spirit strengthens us to be holy (v. 13). He revitalizes us (v. 11). He reminds us that we are God's children (v. 16) and that we are on intimate terms with God (v. 15). He is the firstfruits (v. 23), the guarantee of full salvation to come. He is the informed intercessor who prays for us (vv. 26–27).

How aware are you about the ministry of the Holy Spirit in your life? Do you recognize His work as outlined?

Do you thank God that the Holy Spirit has been given to you because of the work of Jesus? Note the two great blessings of salvation stated in Acts 2:38.

Day 23

Read Romans 8:28–39

Suffering, groaning, and a sense of our own ignorance surround us. Is there any order to the seeming chaos of life?

Paul answers "Yes" in verse 28. God is at work in all things for our good. However, Paul limits this principle in two ways.

The first limitation is by reference to the identity of those for whom God works: they are described as those who love God and who have been called by God. This is not some universal principle that things just have a way of turning out well. No, God works in all things to turn them to the good of His own people.

Paul limits the principle, secondly, by defining the good for which God works (v. 29). He takes us to eternity past to show that in God's foreknowledge, before we existed, God knew us as His own. His knowledge initiated the relationship. It is not as though God knew we would choose Him and then fitted in with our choice; rather, to those who were thus known, God gave a destiny that they should be like Jesus (v. 29). Becoming like Jesus is the good for which God works. It is not our health, comfort, and wealth, but our godliness which He promises to achieve.

In other words, God's purpose is to build a family like Jesus. Jesus is the firstborn, the one in unique relationship with the Father, and He is also one of us because He is the firstborn brother.

Is our conformity to the image of our elder brother guaranteed? How do we know the glory referred to in 8:17, 18, and 21 will be ours? Paul says in verse 30 that it is as sure as the eternal purposes of God; for just as God has predestined us, called us, and justified us, so He will glorify us. Paul places glorification, a future experience, in the past tense to underline its certainty. As God has completed the first three, so will He complete the last, our glorification.

These are such comforting truths. We are spiritual rulers; there is nothing we will meet today that we do not reign over. Nothing can come our way that is not ultimately good for the health of our soul. God will be at work in everything we meet today so that it is for our good, making us like Jesus. This is most comforting news for us, and most frustrating for our enemies.

Do you trust that the sovereign God is at work in your life?

How have you looked for His invisible hand in all things?

Read Romans 8:28–39

The well-known nineteenth-century preacher C. H. Spurgeon said the doctrine of election is one of the most "stripping doctrines in all the world." It is humbling. It means that our salvation began with God. This is the plain teaching of the Bible, yet we don't like to be humbled, so we reject talk of election.

Wherever the New Testament talks about election, it is always in the context of the great blessings we have. Election is a reminder that we should not get big-headed about these blessings. It is not because of us but because of Him that we are His and enjoy such blessings.

Paul concludes this first section of Romans by asking and answering four questions about our security:

- Verse 31: Is there any enemy who can effectively defeat us? No, since God is for us! In giving His own Son, God has shown the extent of His support.

- Verse 33: Is there any lawyer who can effectively make a charge stick against us? No, God has irrevocably declared us to be in the right with Him!

- Verse 34: Is there any accuser who can effectively condemn us? No,

Jesus, who is constantly at God's right hand, will always silence any accusation!

- Verse 35: Is there anyone or any situation that can effectively separate us from God's love? No. Paul lists all the possibilities: no person in the created order, no situation, no extremity—nothing can separate us from the blessings of our salvation in Christ and from God's loving oversight in all these things. Paul concludes that we are super conquerors because of God who loved us (v. 37).

Paul pushes language to its extreme here. At this point, one feels sorry for his notetaker, Tertius (16:22)!

What a magnificent conclusion to the first part of the book. Theologian J. I. Packer identified his favorite chapter in the Bible as that which begins with "There is now no condemnation" and ends with "nor anything else . . . will be able to separate us from the love of God."

No condemnation. No separation. That is momentous news.

Think about your eternal security. How safe are you? (See John 10:27–30.)

Should such security cause you to be careless? (See Hebrews 3:12–15; 4:6–7; 6:4–6.)

Day 25

Read Genesis 3 and Romans 8

These chapters represent the low and high points of human experience. Humanity disobeyed God's clear instruction (Genesis 2:16–17), and as a result, separation and friction entered our experience.

Adam and Eve sensed a separation between each other; their sense of openness was lost (3:7). The man blamed God (3:12) and the woman blamed the snake (3:13).

The man and woman hid from God; their glad fellowship was gone (3:10).

Their environment was going to be against them. Adam would have to deal with weeds (3:18), and Eve would have to handle pain in giving birth (3:16).

They would both find friction in their relationship. She would seek to assert herself over him, and he would seek to despotically rule her (3:16).

They would both face the inevitability of death (3:19), which is part of God's curse upon them. They said to God, "We want paradise, we don't want you," and God expelled them from paradise (3:23–24). Ever since then, we have all lived in a post-Eden environment.

The valley of friction, separation, and condemnation is matched by the peak of no condemnation and no separation of Romans 8.

In Romans 8, we find substantial restoration and fellowship with God, but we still face an antagonistic environment that causes us to groan (8:22–23) as we await the return to the Eden paradise we lost because of sin. We have received the downpayment (here and now, in the person of the Holy Spirit) on all we will receive, there and then (8:23).

Why can this restoration occur? It is all because of the work of Jesus Christ, described in three words in Romans 3:24–25: "justified," "redemption," and "sacrifice of atonement."

Paul never lets us forget that we are not self-made people. We know substantial restoration, and we have the hope of heaven because of the work of Jesus. These blessings cannot be ours apart from that work. They are for believers only; they are only for the children of Abraham.

Note how Paul
underlines in
these verses that
what we have is ours
because of Jesus:
Romans 3:22, 26;
4:24–25; 5:1, 9, 11,
21; 6:23; 7:24–25; 8:1,
34, 39. What are the
implications of this
truth for your faith?

Read Romans 9:1–29

Paul's elated confidence at the end of chapter 8 now turns to "great sorrow and unceasing anguish" (v. 2) as he thinks about Israel's obstinate resistance to the gospel. Does this represent a failure of God's faithfulness to keep His promises to save Israel, or a failure of His Word (v. 6)? The answer is "no." God always intended to save a remnant of Israel. Even among Abraham's children, He chose Isaac, and not Ishmael; Jacob, and not Esau (vv. 7–13).

Does this election mean that God is unjust? (v. 14). No, says Paul. It is not a justice issue. All deserve condemnation. God is sovereign in the exercise of His mercy and in the exercise of whom He hardens, like Pharaoh (vv. 15–18).

If human unbelief is a result of God's hardening of the human heart, why does God still hold us responsible (v. 19)? Such an argument is the equivalent of clay complaining to the potter about the use to which it is put. The potter makes different vessels out of the same lump of clay (vv. 20–21).

Why does God act like this? Why doesn't He just elect everyone? He did this to glorify Himself (vv. 22–24). The unbeliever by his stubborn resistance elevates God's patience; the believer by his undeserved acceptance elevates God's mercy.

Paul then quotes Hosea and Isaiah (vv. 25–29) to show that it was always God's intention to save a remnant of both Jews and non-Jews.

Those who love the Bible but have a problem accepting the doctrine of election will have an obvious problem here. It is an affront to pride to be told that we made no contribution to our own salvation. Salvation is based solely on the electing mercy of God. It is totally undeserved.

Preacher C. H. Spurgeon said this is the "most comforting doctrine of all." Rejection of this truth robs both God of the sole glory due to Him for our salvation, and the believer of the "sweet, pleasant and unspeakable comfort" that comes from knowing our salvation is God's decision and He will never change His mind.

Here is the antidote to every vestige of self-righteousness: **There is nothing for us to feel superior about, for God chose us despite ourselves, not because of anything we have done.** Here is the great motivation for prayer and evangelism: God has an elect people, but we don't know who they are (Acts 18:10). We must take the gospel out in the assurance that God knows who they are, and He will call them to faith when they hear the gospel.

Why should God's unconditional choice of the church surprise us, since He chose Israel unconditionally?

Do you think we have a problem with the teaching of Romans 9 because it is hard to understand, or because it is hard to accept?

Read Romans 9:30–10:21

Two images are used here of Jesus. The first is that of "a rock that makes them fall" (9:33), and the second is "the culmination of the law" (10:4).

Israel stumbled over Jesus. They did not recognize that the law was pointing forward to Jesus, and they treated the law as the means of their salvation instead of finding their refuge in Him.

Paul's anguish for Israel is because his countrymen had chosen the wrong path. They chose to pursue righteousness by obeying the law (9:31; 10:3) and did not submit to God's way of setting people right with Himself.

Verse 2 tells us that although Israel is sincere and zealous (qualities necessary for correctness in this postmodern world), yet she is wrong. For despite her zeal, Israel is ignorant (v. 3).

Paul sets out the two possible routes to righteousness in verses 5 to 7. In verse 5, righteousness is gained by keeping the law. In verses 6 to 7, righteousness is gained not by human achievement but by God's provision. Christ does not need to be brought down (v. 6), but He came down in the incarnation. He does not need to be brought up (v. 7), but He came up in the resurrection. Both of these are God's provision and God's gift of righteousness, and not a result of human achievement.

All religions in one way or another can be categorized as achievement-based. Biblical Christianity alone is categorized as provision-based. **Righteousness is something God requires and provides to all who put their faith in His Son.** Having faith in Jesus means having a particular conviction about Jesus—that God has raised Him from the dead (v. 9). And what the heart believes, the mouth confesses—that He is indeed Lord and God in the flesh (designated as such by His resurrection from the dead, see 1:4).

In verse 11, Paul quotes Isaiah, saying that anyone who has this conviction and confession of Jesus will never be shamed, and that God only has this one way of putting people right with Himself. In verses 12 and 13, he says it is the same for everyone, Jew or Gentile. Everyone who calls on the name of Jesus as God, because of His resurrection, will be saved.

This is indeed momentous news. Think of all those who labor under the burden of religion, striving to meet the requirements of the law in order to be righteous. Whether it is the Christian religion or not, it is equally tragic. It is an impossible task to achieve God's righteousness by law-keeping, and it is totally unnecessary, because Christ, our substitute, has met God's righteous requirements on our behalf. Religion is doubly tragic—impossible and unnecessary.

Why is righteousness by provision, rather than achievement, such good news?

St. Augustine prayed, "O God, demand what you will, but supply what you demand." What does God demand? How does He supply this demand?

Day 28

Read Romans 9:30–10:21

Since faith in Jesus is the way of righteousness, and since God is sovereign in the choosing of His elect, how does God call His elect to Himself? Paul's thinking is very structured at this point. Notice what he says:

Those who call on the name of the Lord will be saved (10:13).

How can they call without belief? (v. 14)

How can they believe without hearing? (v. 14)

How can they hear without preaching? (v. 14)

How can they preach unless they are sent? (v. 15)

Hence, the feet of those who preach such a momentous message are beautiful (v. 15).

Not all who hear the message necessarily believe; not all will be saved. But God is actively calling out His people through the hearing of the gospel (vv. 16–17).

Question 65 of the Heidelberg Catechism—a sixteenth-century document that teaches Christian doctrine—asks, "It is by faith alone that we share in Christ and all His blessings: where then does that faith come from?" Answer 65 responds,

"The Holy Spirit produces it in our hearts through the preaching of the holy gospel . . ."

Didn't Israel hear (v. 18)? Certainly they did. The apostles took very seriously their responsibility of taking the gospel first to the Jews.

Didn't they understand (vv. 19–21)? They understood grace well enough to be jealous of others' reception of it (v. 19). God is sovereign in this process (v. 20), but Israel is personally responsible for her disobedience and obstinacy (v. 21).

The doctrine of election is often attacked because it is said to render the believer paralyzed at the point of evangelism. Not so, says Paul (vv. 1, 17). This doctrine provides the greatest motivation for evangelism. We are not to be put off by people's resistance. **Our confidence in evangelism does not rest on our ability to explain or people's ability to understand, but rests on God's mercy.** That is why prayer must accompany the clear, widespread presentation of the gospel, as the sovereign God does His work of calling out His people as the gospel is explained.

Is the preaching spoken of in verse 15 a particular calling? Strictly speaking, no. However, the preacher needs to know that he is sent and commissioned by God. (See Matthew 9:38 for a similar emphasis.)

ThinkThrough

What is the logic behind each of the steps Paul mentions in verses 11 to 15?

How do these truths challenge your commitment to supporting the widespread preaching of the gospel?

How can you encourage preachers and evangelists today?

Day 29

Read Romans 11:1–10

Paul, a Jew himself, is an example of the fact that God has not abandoned Israel (v. 1). God has always reserved a remnant who will never be abandoned. Paul, Elijah, and the 7,000 who had not bowed the knee to Baal (see 1 Kings 19:10, 14, 18) are examples of that (Romans 11:4). Similarly, at the present time, Paul says there is a small remnant within Israel (v. 5). This remnant is chosen by grace, not by merit (vv. 5–6).

Israel's resistance and blindness are no surprise to God. In fact, "God gave them a spirit of stupor" (v. 8), an insensitivity to revelation. It is God's judgment upon their refusal to heed the gospel. The darkening of their spiritual eyes (vv. 9–10) has overtaken them all, except for the faithful remnant.

Quoting Deuteronomy 29 and Psalm 69, Paul shows that Israel's resistance and blindness are the verdict of Scripture, and that God superintends all this activity. But what is God's purpose in all this? Is this hardening permanent? No (v. 11). Bible commentator Charles Hodge says, "The rejection of the Jews is not total, neither is it final."

We see this pattern repeated in the book of Acts. The gospel comes to the Jews first, then upon their rejection it goes to the Gentiles who accept it, and Israel becomes envious of God's blessing upon the Gentiles (v. 11). Paul therefore makes much of his ministry to the Gentiles, for this is a means of arousing Israel to envy and bringing her to her senses (vv. 13–14). In the economy of God, Israel's stumbling is the means of bringing many Gentiles to Christ.

In verse 16, Paul uses two metaphors: dough in baking and the root and branch of a tree. The principle is that if one part is holy, then the whole batch of baked goods, or the tree, is holy. Therefore, if the firstfruit or root is the Lord's, then the rest is His as well. Hence, if the patriarchs are God's, then those who follow them—elect Israel and elect Gentiles—are His as well. And if Paul and his fellow Jewish believers are the Lord's, then all who follow them with faith in Christ are the Lord's as well.

These are difficult verses. However, we can see that God has a plan and He is working it out. He is the great superintending evangelist, working out the salvation indicated in verse 26. Trusting Him does not lead us to inactivity, but to the activity indicated in Romans 1:14–16.

What do you think about God's ongoing purpose for the Jews?

Should we be especially supportive of evangelism among Jews? Why?

Day 30

Read Romans 11:11–36

The gospel always quells human pride and arrogance. God is attracted by our weakness and repelled by our pride. Gentiles should not be proud, for just as God did not spare Israel because of her unbelief, He will not spare unbelief in those branches that have been grafted in (vv. 17–21)—that is, the Gentiles.

God is both kind and stern. If He is able to graft a wild branch, like the Gentiles, into the tree, then He is more than able to regraft the natural branches (Israel) when they believe in Christ (vv. 22–24).

The mystery (referred to in Ephesians 1:9–10 and 1 Thessalonians 4:13) is now revealed. God is at work through the hardening and softening of hearts to bring the full number of Gentiles into His kingdom, so that "all Israel [that is, all the elect Jews and Gentiles] will be saved" (v. 26). Therefore, the hardening of ethnic Israel is both temporary and purposeful.

This means there is a place in God's purpose for ongoing evangelism among both Jews and Gentiles.

- Jewish resistance
- Gentile belief
- Jewish envy
- Full number of Gentiles has come in
- All Israel (believing Jews and Gentiles) are saved.

Additionally, this may also mean that in the end times (v. 15), we might well see the widespread turning of Jews to Jesus as the Christ. God's purpose is to be merciful to Jews and Gentile alike (vv. 30–32).

Verses 33 to 36 are a final doxology that closes chapters 1 to 11. God's wisdom and knowledge are beyond ours. It is not a result of our advice. God is in no way indebted to us. He is the originator of all things—"from Him"; the director of all things—"through Him"; the object of all things—"to Him" (v. 36).

One writer states, **"The leading principle is that God is the source of all good; that in fallen people there is neither merit nor ability; that salvation consequently is all of grace, as is sanctification, pardon, election, and glory."** For from Him and through Him and to Him are all things. To Him be glory forever and ever. Amen!

Reflect on God's merciful dealings with you.

What is mercy? How has God shown you mercy?

In what ways does this passage encourage you to be humble?

Day 31

Read Romans 5:1; 8:1; 12:1

Paul uses the word "therefore" on three occasions in his letter to the Romans to signal a pause in his argument and to apply his teaching to the lives of his readers.

Having established that righteousness is both God's requirement and God's provision (3:21–26) and that this is nothing new, as demonstrated in the experience of Abraham (chapter 4), Paul comes to his first conclusion in 5:1: "Therefore, since we have been justified through faith . . ."

God's provision of righteousness through faith has three benefits:

1. We have peace with God because of what Christ has done (5:1);

2. We have access, by faith, into an undeserved and unconditional relationship with God, in which we now stand (5:2a);

3. We have an assured future: the glory of God (5:2b).

Paul goes on to show how God's love proves the certainty of that future. His love is seen in the gift of the Holy Spirit (5:5) and the gift of His Son (5:6–8). Righteousness that is provided by God shows itself in our lives as a concern for practical holiness. It is union with Jesus which brings about

justification and which produces sanctification, the necessary fruit of that new life (6:14).

The battle against the old sinful nature, outlined in chapter 7, leaves Paul with two questions: Will he be condemned by his own lack of holiness? And does God leave us under-resourced in this battle against the sinful nature? The first of these is answered by the next "therefore" in 8:1: "Therefore, there is now no condemnation for those who are in Christ Jesus."

Our poor performance will not condemn us because of what Christ has done. The old covenant law of Moses condemned us because none of us could keep it (v. 3), but God sent His Son to fulfill the righteous requirement of the law and to become a sin offering in our place (vv. 3–4). We dread no condemnation now, not because of our record, but because of Jesus's work.

Paul outlines God's purpose to preserve a remnant people for Himself, made up of both Jews and non-Jews. This remnant belongs to God because of the sovereign exercise of His mercy (9:14–15; 11:25–27). In response to these mercies of God,

Paul comes to his last "therefore." In Romans 12:1, we read: "Therefore, I urge you, brothers and sisters, in view of God's mercy, to offer your bodies as a living sacrifice . . ." This, he says, is the fitting response to what God has done in adding us to His remnant people.

ThinkThrough

How often do you take time to reflect on God's mercy in your life and your response to it?

What are the blessings of God's mercies in your life? Give thanks.

Day 32

Read Romans 12:1–2

The biggest challenge a believer faces in his thinking is to keep on recognizing that God's mercy is not a result of human achievement. It is so natural, given the conditional nature of human love and acceptance, to think that God's love and acceptance is also conditional. We need to keep correcting our thinking to see that we are not working to achieve and maintain God's mercy but, rather, to respond constantly to His mercy.

Mercy is always a precondition. It is never a human achievement. Mercy is the environment from which Paul's urging springs (v. 1).

Paul comes to his third great "therefore" in Romans (see 5:1; 8:1; and now 12:1). In view of God's merciful dealings with us, there is an "appropriate" or "reasonable" response, that is, to "offer your bodies as a living sacrifice." Just as the old covenant believer would bring an animal sacrifice in order to maintain a right relationship with God, we are to come as living sacrifices as a reasonable response to the unconditional relationship we have with God, which He has mercifully established.

All the Old Testament sacrifices anticipate the final, central sacrifice of Jesus on the cross. His death makes the Old Testament sacrificial system redundant. It is superseded by Christ's once-and-for all sacrifice on the cross, just as an old currency is superseded by the introduction of a new currency system. However, His death makes the other New Testament sacrifice—the sacrifice of yourself—totally reasonable. And Paul says that this reasonable response is both holy and pleasing to God.

There are things that God takes no pleasure in, like sin and the death of the wicked, and there are things that God takes pleasure in. When Eric Liddell, winner of the men's 400-meter race at the 1924 Summer Olympics, was asked why he kept running, he responded, "When I run, I feel His pleasure."

You can know God's pleasure today as you live fittingly by offering your body to Him as a living sacrifice. In 2 Corinthians 5:15, Paul wrote, "And he died for all, that those who live should no longer live for themselves but for him who died for them and was raised again." Recognizing Christ's purpose for dying and living consistently with it is eminently reasonable.

Hymn writer Isaac Watts puts it this way:
  Love so amazing, so divine,
  Demands my soul, my life, my all.

And missionary C. T. Studd states a similar thought:
"If Jesus Christ be God and died for me, then no
sacrifice can be too great for me to make for Him."

ThinkThrough

Think about how
Paul passionately
urges us, but note
that his appeal is
to our reason.

Why do you think
God is pleased
with you as a living
sacrifice?

Are you living
reasonably in line
with Romans 12:1–2,
or foolishly in line
with the world's
dictates?

Day 33

Read Romans 12:1–2

Paul describes in verse 2 what it means to be a living sacrifice. He gives us the dos and don'ts. First, "Do not conform to the pattern of this world." Or, as Bible commentator J. B. Phillips puts it: "Don't let the world squeeze you into its mold."

The world judges the reasonable response of verse 1 as foolishness. It tells us that to offer ourselves as living sacrifices is being fanatical. Paul says we must not share the world's assessment. Rather, we are to be transformed by the renewal of our mind.

In verse 1, we are told of the reasonable response to God's mercy. Now, in verse 2, we are told that transformation comes via renewal of the mind. The world's view of the self is that self is good. It is to be nurtured, polished, bragged about, and asserted. Paul makes it clear in Romans that we are to assert about ourselves what the gospel asserts about us. See his self-description in 1:1 and how he describes the believers in 1:6–7.

The first command in Romans comes in 6:11, and it is to do with the mind: "Count yourselves dead to sin but alive to God in Christ Jesus." Here, "count yourselves" is the verbal form

of the "reasonable response" of 12:1. Paul's line of thinking looks like this:

- **Renew the mind**
- **Think about self the way God does**
- **Transformed lifestyles as a result**
- **Your body as a living sacrifice to God.**

In Romans 1:21 and 28, Paul says that a fruit of humanity's lack of relationship with God is futile thinking and minds which are depraved or scrambled, unable to make proper moral judgments. That is the typical characteristic of the mind of a natural person. But in Romans 12:2 we see the reversal of that characteristic. The believer has a renewed mind, and that mind recognizes and approves God's "good, pleasing, and perfect will."

Christians are human beings who are human "becomings" in the process of change and on the way to perfection— our eternal state. This change comes via the renewal of the mind and in response to the mercies of God.

How are you living today? Are you living reasonably as a living sacrifice to God, or unreasonably as your own person, doing your own thing, by and for yourself?

What is foolish living? What is reasonable living? How are you living? How will you live reasonably today?

The world says that "living sacrifices" are fundamentalist freaks. But you know that being a "living sacrifice" is the only reasonable way to live for a person who is dead to sin but alive to God in Christ.

A servant is like an oxen waiting for his master's direction. Will it be as a dead sacrifice on the altar, or as a living sacrifice pulling the plough?

Read Romans 12:3–8

When a person comes to Christ, he or she becomes part of a fellowship, a family, a community of God's people. Thus, Paul's first directive to the early church is to show how renewed thinking works out in practice within the new family of the church.

But today, such an emphasis is normally found much further down the order of priorities in the discipleship curriculum. Perhaps it is a reflection of the individualism in churches today.

Paul exhorts the believer to think with "sober judgment" (v. 3), according to the giftedness God has given him. Such gifting is contrary to our deserving (v. 6). The believer must think humbly of self, for he or she is part of a body (vv. 4–5). Hence, he or she is not independent but interdependent.

Paul lists various gifts in verses 6 to 8. It is important to note that his gift lists here in Romans 12, in Ephesians 4, and in 1 Corinthians 12 are not identical. There is a great diversity in God's gifting. It is never static, and God may well gift the same person differently in varied spheres of ministry. The fact that Paul uses participles in describing the gifts shows that they are not to lie dormant, but are evidenced as they are used.

Paul lists seven giftings here. In the last three, he describes the disposition with which they are to be exercised. He tells those blessed with the gift of "giving" to be generous and rightly motivated, not for self-aggrandizement; those blessed with leadership qualities, to lead diligently, not to slacken; and those blessed with the gift of showing mercy, to do it cheerfully, not in a grudging way (v. 8).

I once read an article about the elderly in which the author said that elderly people are often dominated by a fear of being a nuisance. Hence, in showing mercy to the elderly, we must take special care to exude cheerfulness, or they may well develop a "death wish" so as not to be a nuisance to anyone any longer.

Here, then, is renewed thinking in relation to the church: Sober, realistic, humble, exercising our gifting in both a joyous and self-effacing way.

How can you discover your gifting? Ask your church leadership what needs to be done, and ask them to direct you into the area of service for which they believe you are gifted. (Don't add to your burdens the task of discovering your gifts—leave that to your spiritual leadership.) Then get out and exercise your gifts to His glory, within the body of which He has made you a part.

According to
Romans 12:4–5, what
are gifts for?

How can you be
more diligent in
the exercise of your
giftedness?

Which of the
seven areas of
ministry most relate
to you, and how
can you apply Paul's
exhortation?

Day 35

Read Romans 12:9–13

In thinking about ourselves in the church, we are to be both sober and humble. In thinking about the church itself, sincere love is the attitude that must dominate. Our love must not have any pretense about it; it must be genuine. It is not "mushy sentimentality," undiscerning in its affirmations, but clinging to and affirming good, and disapproving evil. In the church family, affection and respect for one another are to be ongoing values.

Paul closes this section with three exhortations. Firstly, all this activity is to be driven spiritually (v. 11). Secondly, it must never be lacking in zeal, but "keep the fires of the spirit burning" (J. B. Phillips). These two are energized by the third exhortation: "waiting like slaves upon the Lord" (Knox translation).

Giving ourselves to Christ's service is both the surest fruit of spiritual fervor and the condition of maintaining the glow. Zeal and service are inseparable twins. Similarly, if we are to rejoice in our future hope and be patient in present affliction, we are to be consistent in prayer (v. 12). As service leads to zeal, so prayer leads to joy and persevering patience. Being busy in our service of others and being faithful in prayer are keys to a healthy spiritual disposition.

Additionally, we are to be eager to practice, or literally "persecuting," hospitality (v. 13)—that is, pursuing opportunities to be hospitable to others with the zeal of a persecutor.

Hospitality, or providing a haven for the needy, is the key to sharing; prayer is the key to joyous perseverance; and service is the key to spiritual zeal. All this is involved in being "a living sacrifice, holy and pleasing to God" (v. 1). Such an attitude is eminently practical in our relationships with God's people.

According to Romans 1:25, idolatry is the great lie. Worshiping the god of self is the greatest apostasy. The best friend is one who urges us away from self-seeking idolatry and reminds us that we are living sacrifices, and that as servants, our calling is to serve! When we serve others in the ways outlined in verses 6 to 8, we are showing in the clearest way our true identity in Christ. This is the reasonable response to God's mercies.

Hospitality was important in the first century. Why is it still important today?

How does the connection of zeal and service help you understand the dynamics of Christian living?

Day 36

Read Romans 12:14–21

The Christian is to resist doing what comes naturally when it comes to responding to antagonism and persecution. Our renewed mind will lead us to bless the persecutor and not curse (v. 14), to rejoice when the persecutor rejoices, and to mourn when he mourns (v. 15). It is natural to do the very opposite.

This section is very much like the teaching of Jesus in the Sermon on the Mount (Matthew 5:38–48). Antagonism will come to us inevitably because "the flesh is hostile to God" (Romans 8:7).

Such opposition is hard enough for Christians without them also having to deal with the most debilitating situation—that of disharmony in the local fellowship. We all know that such disharmony from the least expected quarter—within the church—can be more draining on our spiritual resources than the antagonism of the world (v. 16). We need to resist pride, which creates social and intellectual barriers within the church, and to remember that our Lord Jesus is meek and lowly.

Paul continues making clear in verses 17 to 21 that a Christian's response to antagonism is that of nonretaliation.

The believer will always seek to do what is right and good (vv. 17, 21). It may well be that a Christian in an official position of judge, soldier, or policeman will have to bear the sword of justice, but on a personal level, he or she is committed to nonretribution, thereby leaving room for God's wrath (v. 19). Vengeance is God's work, and He doesn't need our help. In 2 Thessalonians 1:6, Paul makes God's justice clear: "He will pay back trouble to those who trouble you."

In verse 20, Paul quotes from Proverbs 25:21–22. Does this mean that our loving response is a way of bringing judgment upon the antagonist? It probably means that our response will bring him to recognize his shameful behavior and repent. Theologian James Moffatt translates this verse as "make him feel a burning sense of shame," while Bible commentator F. F. Bruce comments that our response will "make him ashamed and lead to his repentance."

If the believer is committed personally to nonretribution, how will God bring about justice? Most often God will use the authorities. Hence Paul goes on to talk about the right Christian attitude towards authorities in Romans 13:1–7.

Are you facing
antagonism because
you are a Christian?
Pray that God will
show you creative
ways to respond.

How can you
overcome evil with
good?

In our society,
how might we be
tempted to show
pride and conceit
(v. 16)?

Read Romans 13:1–7

n recent years, we see an upward trend in cynicism among the electorate round the world. Many people do not think highly of politics, politicians, or government. Paul probably had every reason to share this attitude in Nero's Rome. Yet he says that authorities are established by God (v. 1), instituted by Him (v. 2), God's servants (vv. 4, 6), and agents of wrath (v. 4). Therefore, the believer is to submit to authorities (vv. 1, 5), pay their taxes (v. 6), and give them appropriate respect (v. 7).

Paul could have used the word "obey" instead of "submit." By his use of this word, we recognize that there is something voluntary and mutual in the relationship. The state has obligations and so do we. Unlike first-century Rome, we live in a democracy whereby we vote for those who will govern us every three or four years.

Apathy and ignorance of politics can be subtle forms of rebellion against God. We are to vote intelligently, seek truth, and make assessments based on biblical conviction, and not be swept along by the media. We may choose to write to newspapers, lobby for the good, and even join a political party.

Christians have a variety of attitudes towards their governments:

- Ignore them—because we are not of this world or its political system;

- Total adherence to the government —because it is regarded as equivalent to God;

- Rebellion—because the government is deemed as an agent of evil;

- Limited jurisdiction—because the Lord Jesus taught in Matthew 22 that the state and God have appropriate claims on us. However, God's authority and claim over us must always take top priority.

A word of caution is needed here. If you believe you can share the gospel by joining a political party, by all means do so, but don't idealize the party.

All parties, like religious denominations, have something commendable about them, but they are still imperfect human groupings. God is a God of order, and the authority is an instrument of such order. The political party is an instrument of serving human need, just as the denomination is an instrument of serving the gospel's broadcast. When either a political party or denomination ceases to do that and so compromises you by turning you away from doing these things, then it is time to leave, for we have a higher loyalty to God and to His purpose.

Compare the motivation of unbelievers and believers in their thinking about submission to authority. What extra dimension influences the believer in his or her thinking about obeying government and the payment of taxes?

Day 38

Read Romans 13:1–7

In the late eighteenth century, while reading his Greek New Testament, English politician William Wilberforce became a believer. He then read Philip Doddridge's book *The Rise and Progress of Religion in the Soul* and determined that he should retire as a politician in order to be more directly involved in ministry.

Wilberforce's friends, like cleric John Newton, encouraged him to stay on in the House of Commons and to serve the gospel there. He did so and was instrumental in bringing about the abolition of the slave trade in 1807.

Like the Earl of Shaftesbury who came after him, Wilberforce was a social reformer who worked to establish education for the poor. In fact, many improvements in the fields of health, education, and social welfare, which we take for granted today, can be attributed to the work of these Christian politicians of nineteenth-century England. We should pray for more of such gospel-focused people who will seek to serve the gospel's interests with integrity from within our national, regional, and local governments.

The crucial elements of Wilberforce's spirituality were daily self-examination, prayer, morning and evening devotions, an expectancy of heaven, and a recognition of the importance of solitude.

I raise these godly disciplines here because, **if we are to cope and be fruitful as God-honoring believers in all the circumstances of our busy lives, then we must seek time to think, to renew the mind, and for solitude to reflect on what the gospel says about God and grace, and about ourselves as living sacrifices.**

Without such solitude, reflection, and renewal, which were so vital to Wilberforce and others, we won't experience transformed living and will be sucked along by the proud, apathetic, cursing, vengeful, and cynical world.

How important to you is taking time to think and reflect?

How can you more consistently spend time on quiet reflection?

Read Romans 13:8–14

This section provides one of Paul's more direct references in Romans to the future coming of Christ. His exhortations are built around verses 11 and 12, "The day is almost here. So let us put aside the deeds of darkness . . ."

The central motivation for the appeal of verses 8 to 10 and verses 13 to 14 is the understanding of the present time: **The day of Christ's appearing, the day of "the redemption of our bodies" (Romans 8:23), the day of judgment, is close.**

Therefore, we are to owe no debts except the ongoing indebtedness of loving one another. Just as seeing someone to whom we owe money reminds us of our debt, so too seeing our fellow believers should remind us of our debt of love to them.

In verses 13 to 14, Paul returns to his "put off . . . put on" language (see Ephesians 4:20–5:2). We are to put off orgies, drunkenness, and debauchery, and to "behave decently" (v. 13). In clear contrast to godless behavior, we are to put on the Lord Jesus Christ and His righteousness. We spare no thought about gratifying the sinful nature, that nature as described in chapters 7 and 8.

Verse 14 is sometimes known as "St. Augustine's verse." The great fourth-century Christian leader describes his experience:

"I felt that I was still the captive of my sin . . . all at once I heard the sing-song voice of a child in a nearby house. 'Take it and read, take it and read' . . . I stemmed my flood of tears and stood up, telling myself this could only be a divine command to open the book of Scripture and read the first passage on which my eyes should fall . . . I seized it and opened it in silence. I read the passage on which my eyes fell: 'not in revelry and drunkenness . . . rather arm yourselves with the Lord Jesus Christ; spend no more thought on nature and nature's appetite' . . . in an instant . . . it was as though the light of confidence flooded into my heart and all the darkness of doubt was dispelled."

Augustine then relates that when he told his prayerful mother, Monica, what had happened, "she was jubilant with triumph and glorified [God]."

We must, like Augustine, make sure we get dressed every day—taking off sin and putting on the righteousness of Christ.

Think about what you should take off today and what it means to clothe yourself with Christ.

In what way is love the fulfillment of the law?

Read Romans 14:1–12

Every church fellowship is made up of people from different backgrounds. Our unity as Christians is a unity in diversity.

The church in Rome was a good example of such diversity. In this church there were believers from Jewish and Gentile backgrounds. The Jewish believers were bound by a law-influenced conscience to observe food regulations (v. 2) and special days (v. 5). The Gentiles had no such scruples.

Paul urged the believers to accept one another and to warmly take each other as companions, just as God had accepted them into His fellowship (v. 3).

Each person is specifically warned in verse 3. The Gentile (the stronger) must not think that he is superior and look down on the tradition-bound Jewish believer (the weaker). Likewise, the Jew must not condemn the uninhibited Gentile by slandering him as worldly. Rather, there is to be warm mutual acceptance. Paul calls these issues that have a tendency to divide "disputable matters" (v. 1). What are these matters?

First, they are the matters listed here: food (v. 2), days (v. 5), and drink (v. 21). "Days" includes the observation of

Sabbath (see Colossians 2:16). Note: If Paul saw the fourth commandment as still binding, he would not have have included it here among the "disputable matters."

Second, they are those matters on which the Bible does not speak, or speaks about in an open way, so as to allow believers to have differing views and yet still be one in Christ. These may include differing views of parenting, schooling, politics, church government, sacraments, or music.

We must be careful to recognize disputable matters and not make every issue an indisputable gospel issue. Making disputable matters indisputable is easy to do and doesn't require a lot of thought, but it is disruptive to fellowship and energy-sapping, and wastes precious time.

We must also be careful not to turn indisputable matters into disputable ones. The confessing church in Nazi Germany did this when it asked Jewish believers not to attend church. It wanted to respect the conscience of the weaker brothers—non-Jewish believers who were Nazis. But such a request turned an indisputable matter—that all believers, whatever their background, are welcome into the fellowship—into a disputable one. We must be sure that in our local fellowship we work hard to maintain unity while respecting our diversity.

The foundation of our fellowship is not found in any cultural, political, or denominational expression, but in the fact that Christ died and rose for us and that we are in Him (v. 9).

ThinkThrough

How can you work to maintain unity in your local church while respecting the diversity of those within the fellowship?

Is your church known for its warm acceptance of all believers?

Day 41

Read Romans 14:1–12

In this section, Paul gives the believers in Rome three reasons why they should warmly accept one another and not split over disputable matters.

First, he says in verse 3, "God has accepted them." Our ongoing acceptance of one another is based on God's once-and-for-all acceptance of us in Christ.

If God has not made an issue a barrier to fellowship with Him, then we must not create more rigid standards than God's and make them a barrier for others to fellowship with us. God accepts us through the gospel (v. 4), so we are to accept one another.

Second, he says in verses 5 to 8 that in disputable matters, each person should develop his own convictions. However, verse 6 tells us that those convictions are to be held "to the Lord." That is, each person must live before God with his conviction.

We are to live under Christ's lordship (vv. 7–8). And if even life and death cannot disturb our relationship with Christ, then minor matters like food, drink, or days should not disturb our relationship to Christ or to His church.

Third, in verses 9 to 12, Paul says in essence: Who are we to judge one another when it is Christ's blood that purchased His church? Every knee will bow to Jesus Christ the Lord, not to us; so we're not to judge one another—that is the Lord's prerogative alone.

These are good words for us to hear in our diverse Christian communities. It is very easy for us to reduce the number of disputable matters, and then to judge one another over issues that may be no more than a cultural preference.

Paul's ambition stated in 1 Thessalonians 4:11 is relevant here: "Make it your ambition to lead a quiet life: You should mind your own business and work with your hands."

The accuser of our brothers and sisters is the devil (Revelation 12:10), and he doesn't need any help from us! The one who will judge us is the Lord Jesus, and He shares that throne with no one.

What disputable issues are you tempted to make indisputable?

What are some indisputable matters you may tend to turn into disputable ones?

How can you tell the difference between a disputable and an indisputable matter?

Read Romans 14:13–23

At our sons' school, a "bullying hotline" used to operate. Concerned parents could use the hotline at any time up to midnight. The school took the issue of bullying very seriously.

The apostle Paul takes theological bullying over disputable matters seriously. In chapter 14, he repeats the encouragement to stop passing judgment. The Roman Christians are to make every effort not to cause one another to stumble. Romans 9:33 reminds us of how the Jews sometimes stumbled over God's way of making people righteous. If people do stumble, we must make sure it is not over disputable matters, but over the indisputable Christ of the gospel.

Paul is convicted that no food is unclean (v. 14). Others may disagree, but Paul doesn't wish to quarrel over this conviction. Rather, he respects the conviction of fellow believers. Paul instructs the believers to practice a sensitive exercise of Christian freedom (as he did in 1 Corinthians 8:4 and 7), which is: Love must guide liberty. In other words, we are to be our brother's keeper. Paul sets forth the following principles:

Love is to control the exercise of liberty (v. 15).

Unbounded freedom leads to stumbling (v. 13), obstacles (v. 13), distress (v. 15), destruction (v. 20), falling (v. 21), and condemning (v. 23). This is a serious issue.

Liberty must be exercised, recognizing the preciousness of brothers and sisters in Christ (v. 15); the preciousness of gospel freedom (don't act in a way that will give it a bad name); that matters of eating are peripheral (vv. 19–21); and that life is about building up, not destroying (v. 20).

Our convictions about disputable matters are not for public display (v. 22).

The basis of all that Paul says is that the conscience-bound brother does not have an objective case. If he did, then the issue would no longer be a matter of freedom.

To sum up: We are to make sure we don't put obstacles in front of our brothers and sisters in Christ, or destroy their faith by the insensitive exercise of our Christian liberty. The kingdom of God is about righteousness, peace, and edification, so we must work for that and keep convictions about peripheral matters to ourselves.

Freedom must be constrained by love.

What are some matters that fall into the category of being disputable today?

How do you show your respect for both your freedom in living under the gospel and for other Christians who may differ with you on these matters?

Day 43

Read Romans 15:1–13

Paul could easily have concluded his remarks at the end of chapter 14, but he keeps on like a dog with a bone. The unity of the church is an important issue.

Today, Christian unity is too expendable. Denominations divide us too easily, and even at the local church level we are far too portable. When there is a difference or offense, we tend to just move to another church.

Christian unity is God-given. It is precious, and we need to work hard to maintain it.

Paul's word in verses 1 to 6 is to the strong. Such people are to take the initiative and bear with those with a tender conscience. In the exercise of freedom, they are to build up their neighbor. That's what Jesus did. He did not please himself but bore the burdens of others. The Old Testament too is full of examples of perseverance, endurance, and God's faithfulness.

Such consideration in the way we live does not come naturally. We need God's help, and that's why Paul wishes God's blessing on them in verses 5 to 6.

In verses 7 to 13, he says that both the strong and the weak are to take the initiative and accept one another.

Jesus again is the model of such acceptance. God doesn't discriminate between the weak and the strong. God's church is not exclusive. God's acceptance of both is the basis of our acceptance of one another.

Again, such acceptance does not come easily to us, so Paul asks God's blessing in verse 13. In this verse there is a strong emphasis on hope. God is the God of hope. And hope causes an overflow of joy and peace. In 1 Thessalonians 1:3, Paul says that the fruit of hope is endurance.

Maintaining unity can be hard work, and we need to keep our eye on the prize. That's what hope does. The prize is heaven, being in the presence of Jesus together with our fellow believers in perfect union.

We need to warmly accept and bear with one another as we live in the light of such hope.

How can the
example of Jesus
encourage you to
live in unity with
believers with whom
you may disagree?

How might you
show that you value
Christian unity only
lightly?

How are you driven
by Christian hope
today?

Day 44

Read Romans 15:14–33

In and of itself, it is neither wrong nor right to be ambitious. It all depends on what you are ambitious for. Ambition for money will make you greedy. Ambition for pleasure will make you indulgent. Ambition for recognition will make you self-promoting.

Paul uses the word "goal" or "ambition" on three occasions: In 2 Corinthians 5:9, in 1 Thessalonians 4:11, and here in Romans 15:20.

This verse is a good reminder that Paul was an incidental theologian—he was first and foremost a missionary church planter. This does not mean that he was theologically sloppy. The letter to the Romans is testimony to his theological acumen. However, it does mean that all of Paul's thinking was to serve the enterprise of taking the gospel where there was no existing church, "where Christ was not known" (v. 20). Like sixteenth-century theologian John Calvin, who studied theology in order to be a better pastor, Paul makes sure that all truth and insight drive his mission endeavors.

How does Paul view his ministry?

First, all he is and does is based on God's grace (v. 15). He never forgot his days as a persecutor of the church.

Second, he is a "minister" of Christ Jesus (v. 16). This word is used to describe serious government service.

Third, his ministry priority (v. 16) is to pass on to the Gentiles the gospel from God in order that their lives would become an offering acceptable to God (see 2 Corinthians 11:8).

Fourth, his ministry is self-effacing (v. 17) and is a result of Christ's accomplishment (v. 18). **Paul is not out to build a following for himself. His ministry is based on grace, focused on the gospel, and undertaken in a self-effacing manner.**

Here are self-evident truths that help us recognize false claims:

• You can't be fit without exercise;

• You can't become wealthy without watching how you spend;

• You can't be slim without watching what you eat;

• You can't grow a true church without the gospel of grace being prominent.

Paul is God's instrument to proclaim the gospel to the Gentiles. Where will this lead him? From Jerusalem in the east to Illyricum in the north-west (v. 19).

What are you
ambitious for today?
Where are your
ambitions leading
you?

How do your
ambitions affect
the gospel and its
ministry?

Day 45

Read Romans 15:14–33

have dwelt for years practically alone in Africa. I have been thirty times stricken with fever, three times attacked by lions, and several times by rhinoceri; but let me say to you, I would gladly go through the whole thing again, if I could have the joy of again bringing that word "Savior" and flashing it into the darkness that envelopes another tribe in Central Africa. —William R. Hotchkiss, missionary in Africa in the nineteenth century.

The apostle Paul expressed a similar ambition in verse 20. Such aspiration will show itself in plans and strategies. After exhausting his church-planting opportunities in the east (v. 23), Paul planned to go west, and Spain was as far west as it was possible to go then. But Paul would first go to Jerusalem (vv. 25–26) with his collection from the Gentile churches to ease the famine there. The Gentiles were glad to contribute to this (v. 26), for since they had shared in their spiritual blessing, the gospel, then likewise they should share materially with believers in Jerusalem.

So Paul's plan was to head to Jerusalem and then to Spain via Rome. Without embarrassment, he asks them to financially support his trip to Spain (v. 24).

Likewise, missionaries today must never feel self-conscious about asking for support for missionary endeavors. Such requests are actually opportunities for believers to make investments for eternity, ensuring that they will be "welcomed into eternal dwellings" (Luke 16:9).

Paul recognized that his plans were in the hands of God and he would come only in the blessing of Christ (v. 29). Paul further recognized that none of our plans can succeed without the blessing of God, so he urged his brothers to prayer (vv. 30–33).

There is to be no vestige of pride or arrogant self-dependence in our planning or strategizing. God is attracted to human weakness and nothing manifests our weakness more than when we call out to God. The Christian life begins with calling on God (Acts 2:21), and so it is to continue in our calling out to God—for apart from Him our plans are meaningless. Nothing so repulses God as human self-sufficiency, pride, and arrogance, which shows itself in our prayerlessness—our lack of dependence on Him.

How valid is it to
make plans for the
future? What are
their limitations?

What does Paul
show here about a
right attitude to the
financial support
of human need
and evangelistic
missions?

Day 46

Read Romans 15:14–33

Paul urges the Romans to literally agonize with him in prayer (v. 30). The word he uses describes a soldier who joins in the defensive line. Such is the nature of prayer: it is seen as part of a battle, a struggle for the gospel.

They are to pray:

- That Paul will be rescued from the belligerent unbelievers in Jerusalem (v. 31);

- That the collection among the Gentile churches will be accepted by the Jerusalem church and thus provide a seal of approval on Paul's Gentile ministry;

- That Paul will then be free to come and join them in Rome for further refreshment. He has already referred to this in Romans 1:11–13.

Paul probably wrote the letter to the Romans during his 18-month stay in Corinth (see Acts 18:11). Luke's record in Acts tells us how these prayers were answered.

According to Acts 21, the Jerusalem church accepted the collection and Paul was delivered from the unbelievers. His deliverance came from the unbelieving Roman garrison (Acts 21:30–32), a most unexpected source.

Did he make it to Rome? Yes, but it was not easy. He came via court appearance, storm, shipwreck, snakebite, and under chains, as the guest of the Roman government. He had appealed to Caesar and so the Romans brought him, under arrest, to Rome. We cannot be certain whether Paul ever reached Spain, as he hoped.

God hears and answers the prayers of His people, but often in unexpected ways.

You may be praying about a matter now, and you can be sure that God hears your prayer. He will answer in one way or another. His answer may well be unexpected, as it was in the case of Paul. Paul follows his benediction about hope (v. 13) with a further benediction about peace (v. 33).

Traditionally, letters of the first century began with wishing their readers peace and prosperity; Paul changed that to "grace and peace" (1:7). Having made it clear that peace and hope are direct results of God's provision of righteousness (5:1–2), it is fitting that Paul should conclude this section of his letter by focusing on these two qualities. Justification reminds us that God's wrath has been spent and He is at peace with us, and that what God has begun in providing us with a righteous standing, He will complete in our glorification. That is our hope.

How important to
your daily life is
Christian hope?

How important is it
to you to know that
God is at peace with
you? Why?

Day 47

Read Romans 16:1–16

In Romans 1:16, Paul said that the gospel is the means used powerfully by God to bring people to salvation. He now lists some of those who have been saved through this powerful gospel.

Paul sends greetings to twenty-seven people, some of whom he names, but he mentions more: the church, the household, the brothers, a mother, a sister, and the saints.

Some of them are men, and some are women. Some have Jewish names like Mary, some have Greek names like Hermes, and some have Roman names like Julia. Some are people of wealth—heads of households like Aristobulus and Narcissus. Some have an obviously close bond with Paul, like Rufus's mother, Andronicus, and Junias. We know some from elsewhere in the Bible, like Priscilla and Aquila (Acts 18:1–3); others we have only heard of their name, like Apollos.

All their work is elevated and reported to be significant, whether it was teaching, as with Priscilla and Aquila, or the hard work of Mary (v. 6), Tryphena, Tryphosa, and Persis (v. 12). We don't know exactly what their work was, but it was recognized and affirmed by the apostle.

The description that dominates this section is "in Christ" and "in the Lord." All of these people have this in common: they were once outside of Christ, but because of the gospel, they were now in Christ and with Christ—in His presence forever, enjoying the fulfillment of their hope.

They knew they were part of God's family: knowing God as Father, Christ as elder brother, and one another as brothers and sisters together in one family. Thus Paul urges them to greet each other as siblings "with a holy kiss" (v. 16).

Paul's words regarding Phoebe in verses 1 to 2 are significant, as it was most likely that she was the carrier of the letter to the Romans. We can thank God for her safe arrival at Rome, her warm reception by the church, and the preservation of this first-century letter that continues to strengthen the church today.

Look at Paul's descriptions of individual Christians in the list. If Paul were to include your name in this list of greetings, how do you think he would describe you?

What do these verses teach about our unity in Christ, the nature of ministry, Paul's relationship with the church, and the power of the gospel?

Day 48

n Bible commentator J. B. Phillips's translation of the Acts of the Apostles, published in 1955, he wrote in the preface: "If [the early Christians] were uncomplicated and naïve by modern standards, we have ruefully to admit that they were open on the God-ward side in a way that is almost unknown today."

Being "open on the God-ward side" is an apt description of the believers in first-century Rome. There was a refreshing unpretentiousness about the early church—their self-sacrifice, the quality of their relationships, and the depth of their commitment are challenges to us all.

However, there is no such thing on earth as a perfect church, and just as Paul has urged previously in the letter (12:2; 15:31), he now urges them to be on guard against those who seek to disrupt the work by providing teaching contrary to the content of the apostolic gospel (v. 17). These are self-serving, smooth-talkers who seek to deceive naïve people. So, Paul urges, "keep away from them" (v. 17). It is a simple and stark instruction.

Paul encourages them to be wise and discerning, yet at the same time to be inexperienced in the matter of evil (v. 19). Such a combination of innocent openness and discerning wisdom is rare. Note that despite everything Paul has taught them about love and respect for one another, it does not mean they depreciate the truth for the sake of love. Apostolic truth is vital and non-negotiable, and must not be watered down so as to be all-inclusive.

Again Paul refers to the God of peace (v. 20), especially appropriate here in the context of friction and division due to the work of the flatterers. He assures them that the God of peace will soon end all of Satan's activity (v. 20). Paul refers to Genesis 3:15, "he will crush your head, and you will strike his heel," when he states that God will "crush Satan under your feet." The victory over Satan is achieved through the death and resurrection of Jesus, but he is further crushed in the personal deliverance of all believers.

As we battle in the midst of strife, we have the hope of final victory and the presence of God's grace to sustain us in the fight (v. 20).

How do you
continually practice
the truths of the
gospel and guard
them against those
who would seek to
depreciate them?

Can you think of
situations where unity
and truth conflict?
Where do your
loyalties lie?

Day 49

Read Romans 16:21–27

Paul now concludes this great letter with greetings from his close co-worker Timothy (v. 21). Tertius, who wrote down the letter at Paul's dictation (v. 22), sends his own personal greeting, and Paul sends greetings from his host Gaius (v. 23). Once again, we have this glimpse of Paul: not the unapproachable, cold, stiffly orthodox apostle, but a man engaged in warm relationships with the churches. We can't help but be impressed by the warmth of his widespread greetings.

He has offered blessings at 15:13, 15:33, and 16:20, but now he comes to his final benediction (vv. 25–27), which is the longest of all his letters. These are memorable last words: "Now to him who is able to establish you in accordance with my gospel, the message I proclaim about Jesus Christ, in keeping with the revelation of the mystery hidden for long ages past, but now revealed and made known through the prophetic writings by the command of the eternal God, so that all the Gentiles might come to the obedience that comes from faith—to the only wise God be glory for ever through Jesus Christ!"

Paul ends as he had begun in Romans 1:1–5. There, the emphasis was on the gospel, promised through the prophets, to the effect that the Gentiles might be called to the obedience which comes from faith. Paul never moves far from the gospel. He never forgets his persecuting past and God's grace in allowing him to come to Christ.

He introduces the gospel, he defines the gospel, he expounds the gospel, and he describes how the gospel transforms. Finally, he commits those who have been powerfully saved by the gospel to the God "who is able to establish you in accordance with my gospel" (v. 25)—that is, the apostolic gospel of God's provision of righteousness in Christ, expounded in this letter.

In his final address to the elders at Ephesus (Acts 20:32), Paul showed similar confidence in God's ability. He appointed elders in each church and "committed them to the Lord, in whom they had put their trust" (Acts 14:23).

God holds, protects, and establishes us through the gospel—the gospel which declares that all those who are in Christ have an eternally unchanging, righteous status with God.

Write out a prayer to God in response to the truth of Romans.

What is "the obedience that comes from faith" (Romans 1:5)? What does such an expression teach us about faith?

Day 50

Read Romans 3:21–26

In summarizing Romans, we return to what is possibly the most important single paragraph ever written, in which Paul announced something of the grandeur of Christ's saving work—God's perfect plan in bringing us, the unrighteous ones, to Him through His Son Jesus Christ, the righteous one.

Think about it: Romans 3:21–26 is more important than a paragraph of Shakespeare, or the economic theory of Karl Marx or Adam Smith, or one of Winston Churchill's famous speeches.

Paul utilizes three words in common use in his day to describe what God has done for us in Christ:

- "Justified" (v. 24): A legal term, whereby God the judge declares the guilty to be in the right with Him.

- "Redemption" (v. 24): A business term. God justifies not on a whim, but on the basis of the work of His Son in laying down His life to buy us back from the bondage of sin.

- "Sacrifice of atonement" (v. 25): A religious word. Jesus, by dying, bears in Himself the just wrath of God on human sin, so that guilty sinners don't need to bear it.

On the basis of the redeeming, atoning work of Jesus, God declares the guilty sinner to be justified. That is, not only is our sin forgiven, but righteousness is also credited to our account. So we stand perfect before God, clothed in righteousness divine. Jesus Christ is the foundation of our righteousness. Faith links us to the work of Jesus our substitute. It is God's gift to us and we have nothing in which to boast (Romans 3:27).

This truth is the heart of Paul's argument and the source of our assurance. All religion, the attempt to somehow win and keep God's favor, is ultimately dehumanizing, reducing people to nervous wrecks. Can we ever do enough? Religion places us on an impossible and unnecessary quest.

This paragraph in Romans tells us that righteousness is not only God's requirement but also His provision. It announces that the Christian faith is nonreligious. It is not about what we must do, but about what God has done.

As such, hymn writer Edward Mote pens: "My hope is built on nothing less than Jesus' blood and righteousness." This is our anthem too!

Think about how good and how reassuring Romans 3:21–26 is for the uncertain adherents of any religion. Is it not worthy of a wider broadcast? How can you be involved in that?

Going Deeper in Your Walk with Christ

Whether you're a new Christian or have been a Christian for a while, it's worth taking a journey through the Gospels of Matthew, Mark, Luke, and John. Each Gospel presents a distinct aspect of Christ and helps us gain a deeper appreciation of who Jesus is, why He came, and what it means for us.

Hear His words. Witness His works. Deepen your walk with Jesus as you follow Him through the wonderful scenes painted in the Gospels.